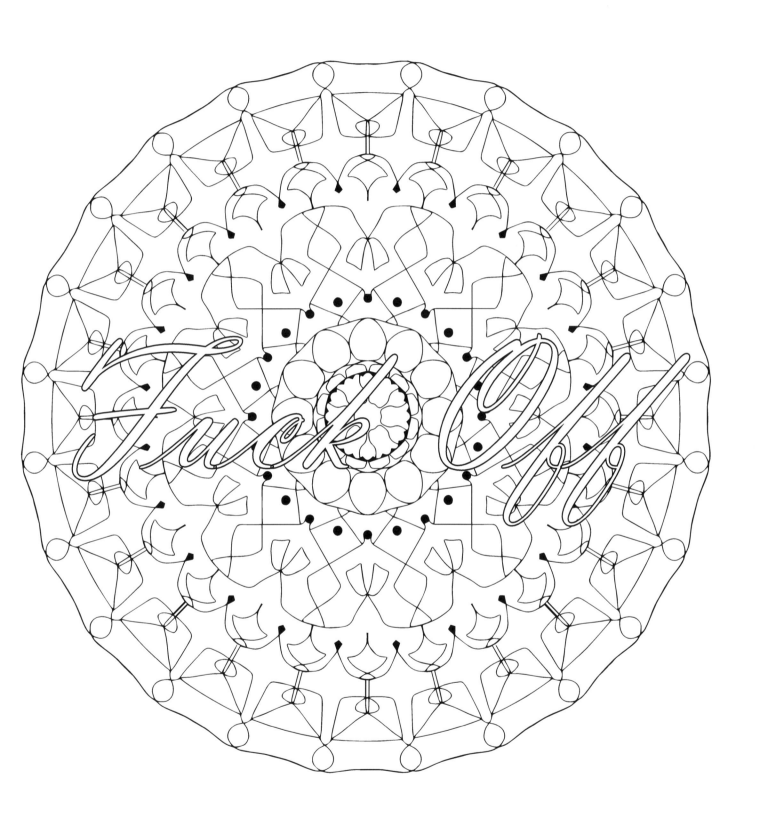

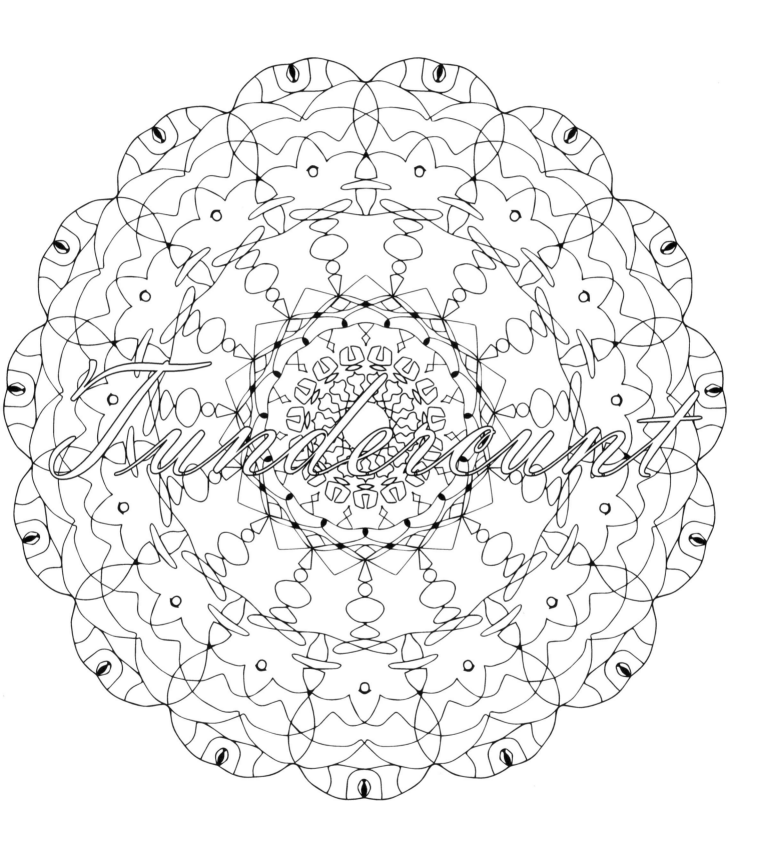

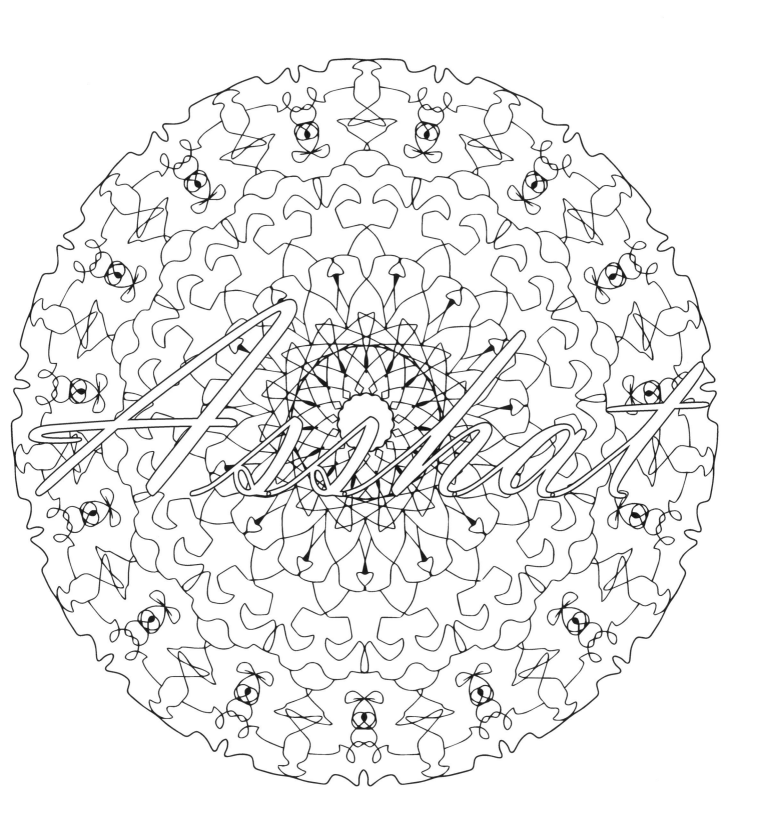

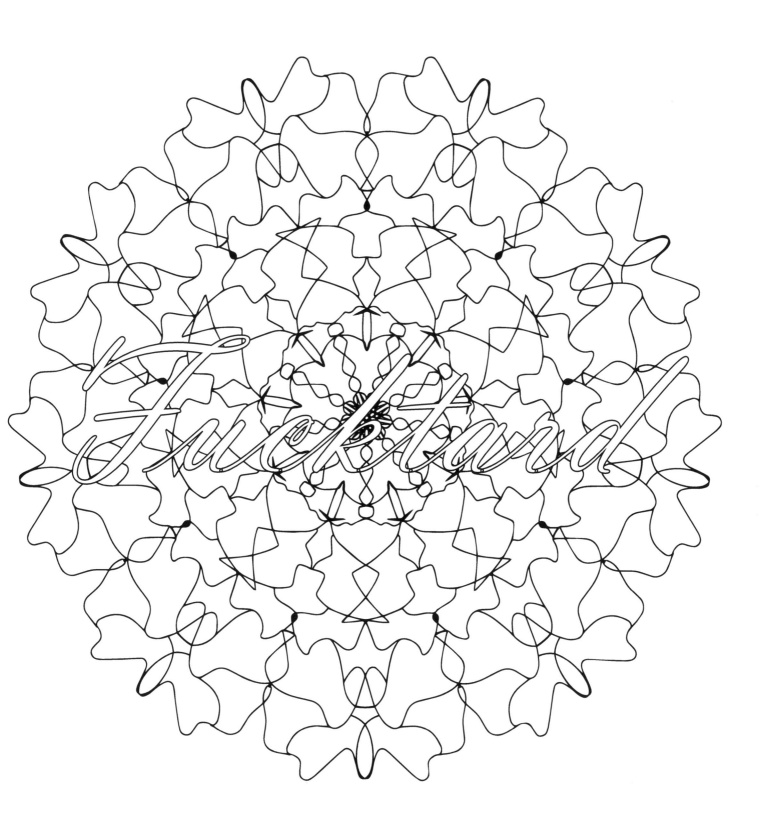

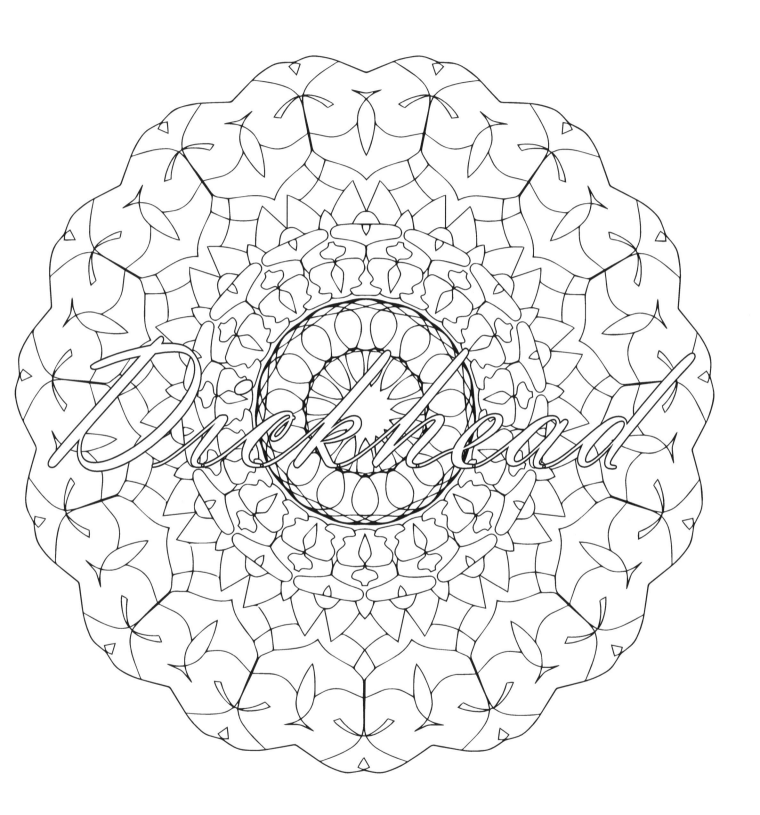

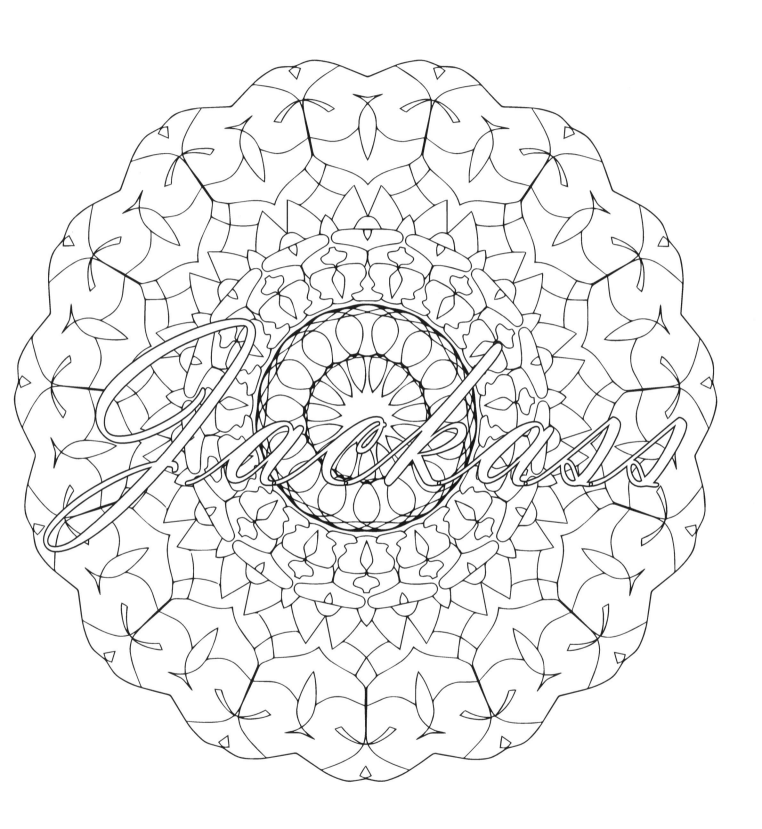

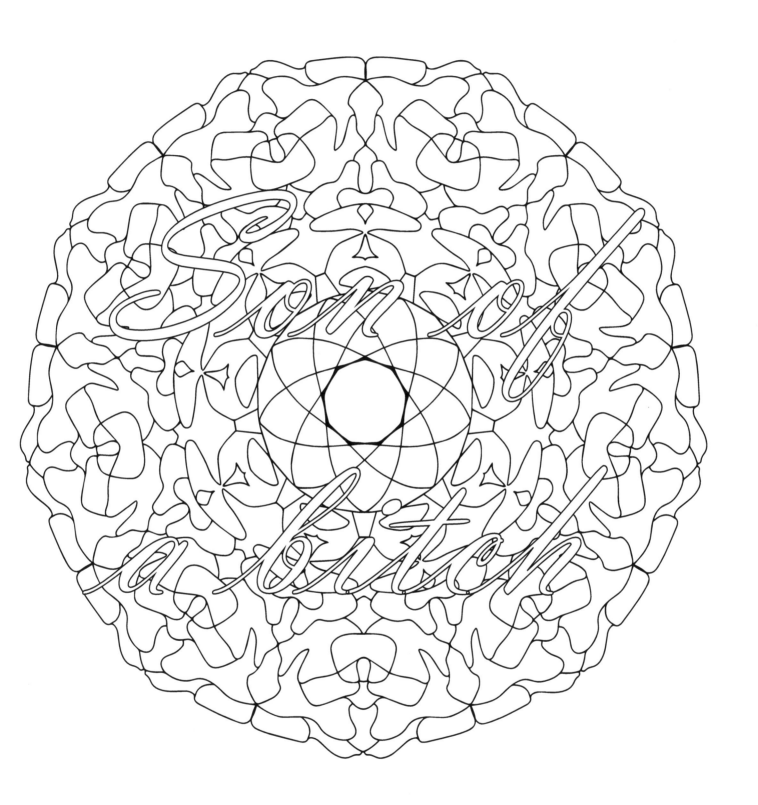

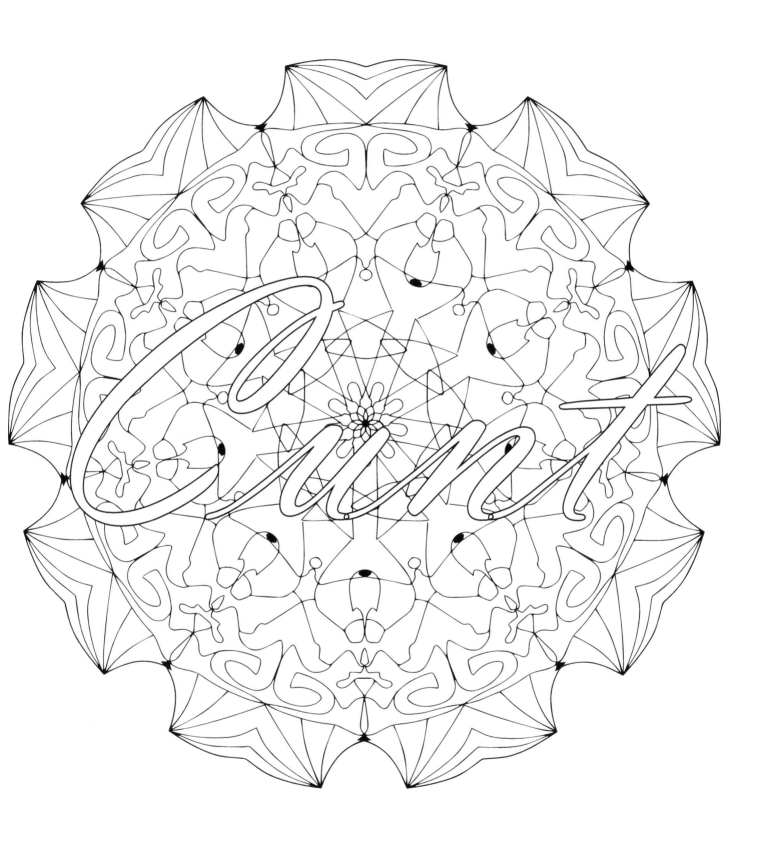

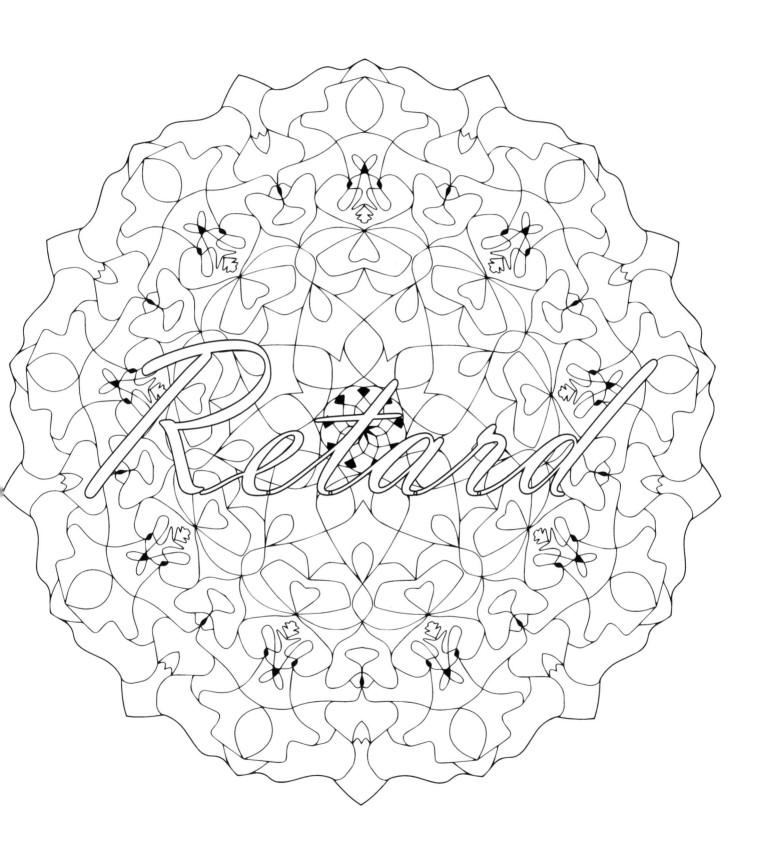

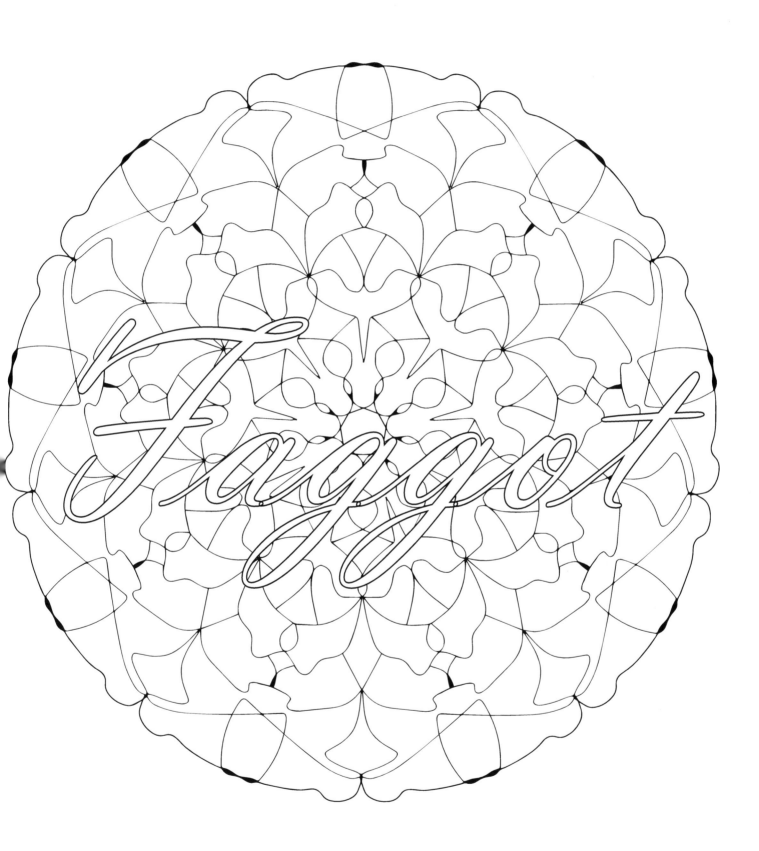

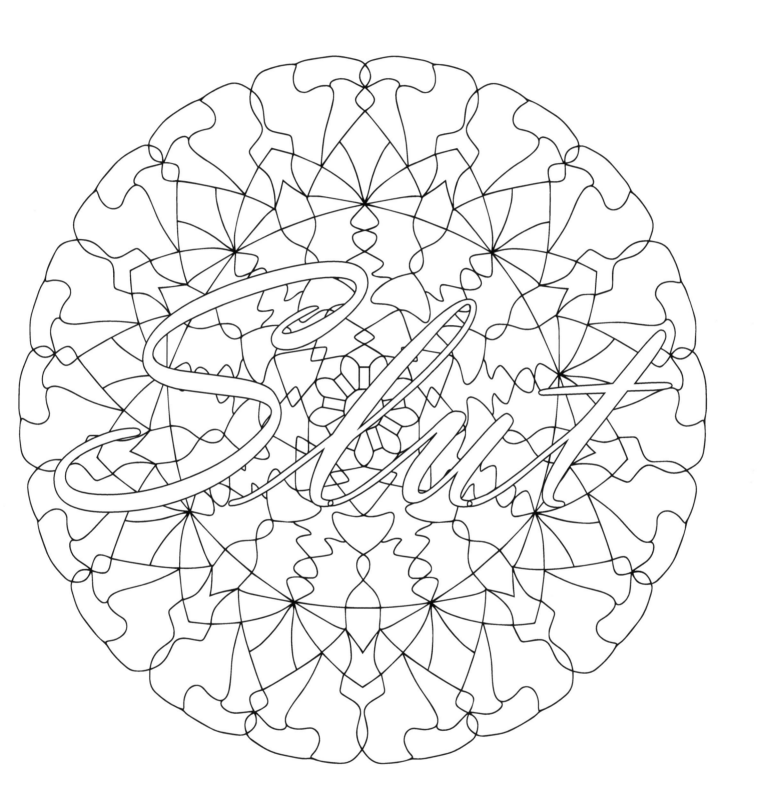

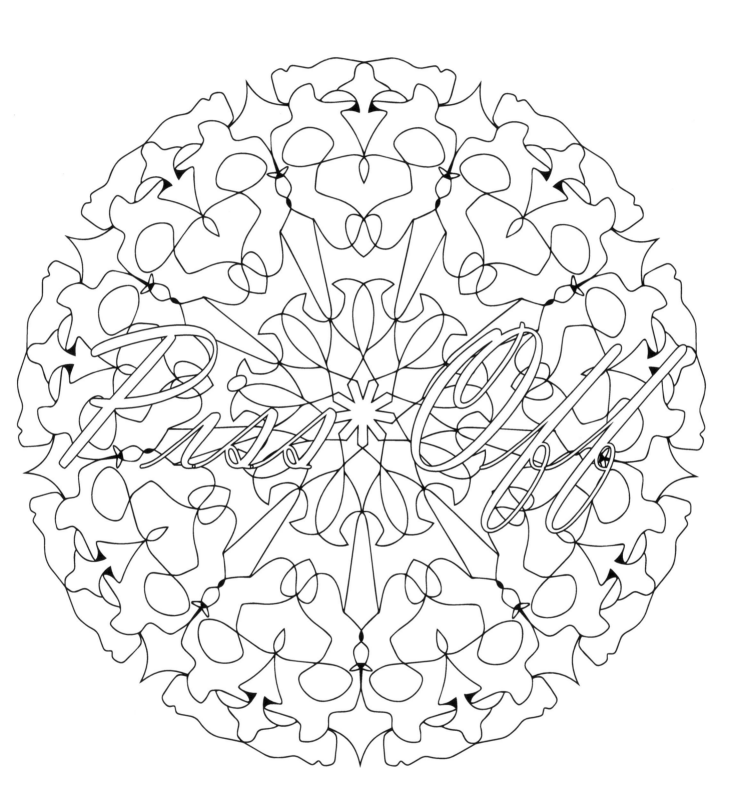

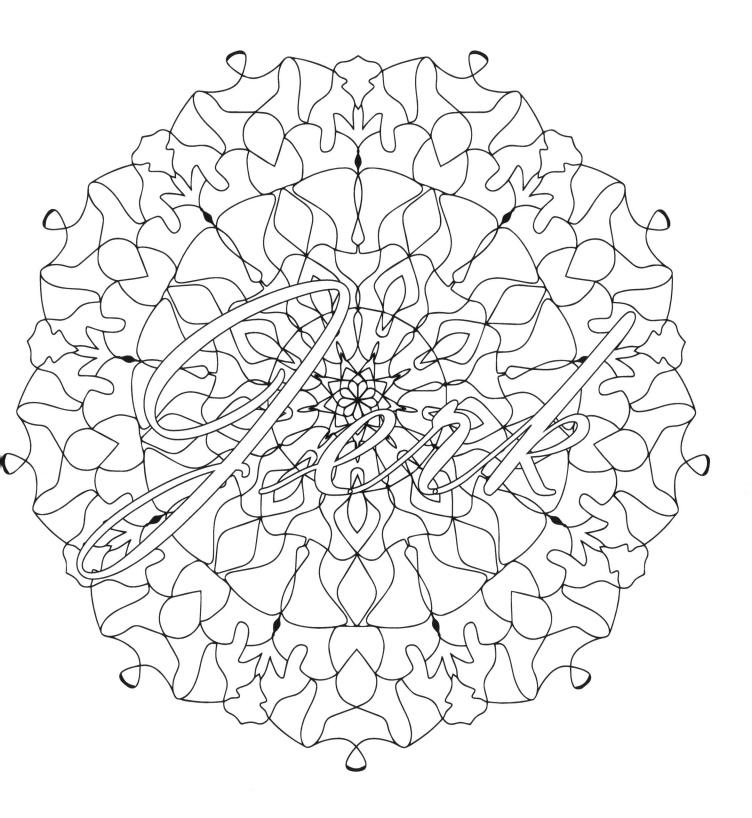

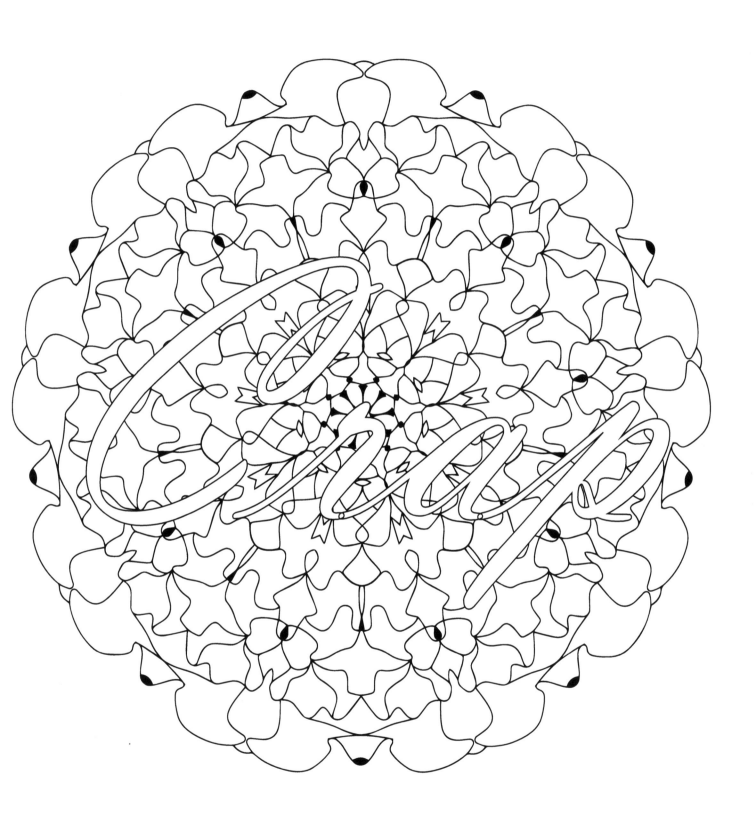

Pallete Test Sheet

Thank You!

We want to thank you for purchasing this book!
If you enjoyed this book, then I'd like to ask you for a favor,
would you be kind enough to leave a review for this book
on Amazon? It'd be greatly appreciated!

Make sure you follow us:
amazon.com/author/unibulpress
facebook.com/adultcoloringpress/
instagram.com/unibulpress/
pinterest.com/unibulpress/

unibulpress.com

If you have colored a page from our book and upload it
to any social media please make sure you tag us or link to
the book :) Thank you again for purchasing!

Printed in Poland
by Amazon Fulfillment
Poland Sp. z o.o., Wrocław

16282908R00043